Simple Handmade Jewell

Simple Handmade Jewellery

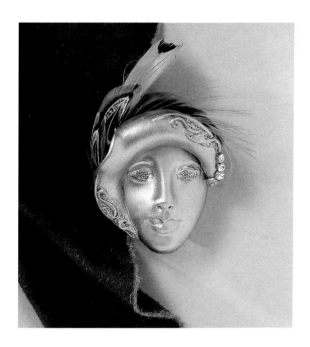

SEARCH PRESS

First published in Great Britain 1993
Search Press Limited,
Wellwood, North Farm Road,
Tunbridge Wells, Kent TN2 3DR

This book has been rewritten and rearranged from illustrations and
material in the following titles of the Brunnen-Reihe series, published in
German by Christophorus Verlag, Freiburg-im-Breisgau: copyright ©
respectively 1987, 1989, 1989, 1990, 1989, 1990, 1990, 1990, 1990, 1991
Christophorus-Verlag GmbH

Aparter Modeschmuck aus Fimo modelliert by Sigrid Elsenhans (BR261)
Modeschmuck – jung, chic, exklusiv im Trend by Renate Bosshart (BR287)
Perlmutt – Modeschmuck im Trend by Michaela Willi (BR299)
Schmuckstücke aus Fimo by Cornelia Rudolph (BR302)
Schmuck Exquisit aus bemaltem Glas by Ingrid Moras (BR303)
Schmuck-Ideen mit Fimo – modisch und elegant by Stephanie Jeep (BR304)
Schmuckträume – Glas und Farbe by Ingrid Moras (BR310)
Modischer Perlmutt-Schmuck by Michaela Willi (BR314)
Schmuck-Variationen: Unikate aus bemaltem Glas by Peter Sacherer (BR329)
Schmuck-Collection – modische Variationen by Cornelia Zorrmann (BR333)

Photographs by Ulrike Schneiders
Translated by Jessica Lysaght

The publishers would like to thank Hobby Horse Ltd., 15–17 Langton
Street, London SW10 OJL, and Redburn Crafts, The Craft Centre, Squires
Garden Centre, Halliford Road, Upper Halliford, Shepperton, Middlesex
TW17 8RU, for checking the specialist jewellery terms used in this book.

If you have difficulty in obtaining any of the equipment or
materials mentioned in this book, please write for further
information to the Publishers, Search Press Ltd., Wellwood,
North Farm Road, Tunbridge Wells, Kent TN2 3DR

ISBN 0 85532 749 9 (pb)
ISBN 0 85532 764 2 (hb)

Printed in Spain by A. G. Elkar, S. Coop. 48012 Bilbao

Contents

Introduction

If you thought that because gold and diamonds were unattainable you had to wear mass-market jewellery, then this book will be a revelation to you. It presents hundreds of ideas to help you create your own handmade jewellery to suit your personal taste, to match your outfits or reflect your favourite colour, or simply to let you wear something totally unique. Designer style without a designer price tag!

The pieces of jewellery are all are easy to make. Some take literally only a few minutes to assemble, whilst others offer you endless possibilities for artistic invention and discovery. Whatever your taste, whether you prefer diamanté, leather, mother-of-pearl, glass, or fantasy forms modelled from clay, you will find something within these pages to inspire you and encourage you to get your creativity going.

Mother-of-pearl jewellery

Fashion jewellery has associations with the positive side of life – the fun of looking lovely without spending a fortune. There are so many pieces to choose from that you can really be creative in making your own jewellery. You need no previous knowledge to start working with mother-of-pearl, as you will soon realize.

Mother-of-pearl is a completely natural material that comes from the innermost layer of sea-shells and snail-shells. For centuries it has been used in the Far East for carvings and inlaid work, and it has also been used in Europe for inlaying, buttons, etc. Because of the shell's thin chalky lamellae, the light breaks in such a way as to form delicate rainbow colours – this gives mother-of-pearl its particular charm.

This section will inspire you to make all sorts of jewellery by combining mother-of-pearl with other materials – you will see just how versatile it can be!

BASIC MATERIALS AND TECHNIQUES

Materials

There are different sorts of mother-of-pearl: 'white shell', which is usually already cut into shapes and polished, and 'abalone shell' (the coloured form), which is also often pre-cut but can be bought in pieces. These broken pieces are best combined with modelling clay, or adapted to make simple earrings if the pieces are big enough.

Equipment

One pair of flat-nosed pliers; one pair of round-nosed pliers; sandpaper; small knife; paintbrush; toothbrush; glue (the sort that bonds metal to metal and to other materials such as mother-of-pearl and modelling clay); hobby drill with a bit with a diameter of 1mm (about ¹/₃₂in) for drilling holes in any pieces of shell which are not pre-drilled.

Techniques

Closing rings For bending and closing rings, use your two pairs of pliers. Hold the ring firmly with one pair and close it with the other. What you are doing will dictate which one you use for which operation.

Joining pieces of mother-of-pearl together Roughen the places where you intend to apply the glue with sandpaper, stick the pieces together, and finish them off with decorative bits and pieces. As soon as the glue is tacky, you can stick the brooch-pins or hair-slides to the back of the mother-of-pearl, but you must wait ten hours before you can wear your jewellery.

Working with oven-bakeable modelling clay Knead the clay well for five to ten minutes before you start. Roll it out with a rolling pin on a flat surface to get flat sheets of clay from which you can cut out shapes such as leaves. If you want thin threads of clay, use a garlic press. You can texturize the surface with netting or a toothbrush, and give leaves fine veins by using little ridged shells. When bronzing the modelled clay pieces, you would normally dab gold or silver powder on the piece before hardening; but when using mother-of-pearl the effects are better if you use other colours, such as red, blue, or green, mixed with silver powder and applied with a brush. This produces some beautiful nuances of colour. Harden the clay in the oven at 100° to 130°C (210° to 260°F) for ten to fifteen minutes. Note that some colours of clay need to be hardened at the *lowest* temperature: always check manufacturers' instructions. If you are using light-coloured modelling clay, keep an eye on it to make sure it does not get too dark or start to turn brown. After hardening, carefully take the piece off the brooch-base, mother-of-pearl or whatever, if you can, and stick it back again with glue. This makes the piece of jewellery last longer. Lastly, varnish the modelled clay pieces to fix the bronzing powder, using matt or gloss special varnish.

You can use modelling clay to fill out hollows or as a base into which you can press pieces of mother-of-pearl, etc. You will find more tips on working with modelling clay on pages 24–5 and 48–51.

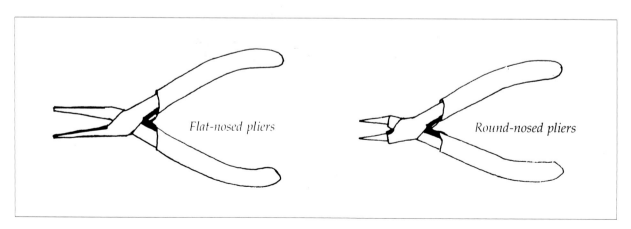

Flat-nosed pliers   *Round-nosed pliers*

INDIVIDUAL PIECES

Golden strands

Materials Three mother-of-pearl shapes; three little 'fringes' of golden strands; chain on which to hang the pendant, about 45cm (18in) to 55cm (22in) long; two tulip-shaped end caps; one spring clasp; one flat loop (if unavailable, bend the edges of a ball cap *outwards* to create a flat surface); three jump rings; two shepherd's-crook ear-wires.

Method With a hobby drill, bore a little hole about 1mm (¹⁄₃₂ in) in diameter in each piece of mother-of-pearl – not too close to the edge, or it may splinter.

For the necklace, roughen the back of one of the mother-of-pearl shapes lightly with sandpaper and attach a flat loop with a drop of glue. Glue the tulip-shaped end caps to the ends of the chain. Leave the whole thing to set for at least five hours, then attach the golden strands to the mother-of-pearl with a jump ring and close the ring using two pairs of pliers. Thread the chain through the flat loop and attach the catch with a pair of pliers.

For the earrings, push the shepherd's-crook ear-wires through the hole and also through the loop that attaches the strands to the mother-of-pearl.

Mother-of-pearl with golden leaves

Materials Three mother-of-pearl shapes (triangular); three leaf pendants; a chain of the required length; two tulip-shaped end caps; a spring clasp; three jump rings; two shepherd's-crook ear-wires.

Method These items of jewellery are assembled in the same way as the necklace and earrings on page 9, except that instead of sticking a flat loop to the pendant, you should use a jump ring to hang the pendant from the necklace.

Variation It is also possible to combine coloured elements with the white mother-of-pearl, such as coloured beads threaded on to brass wire.

Feathers and teardrops

NECKLACE (see above – centre)

Materials One mother-of-pearl shape; one teardrop pearl (small); two small bent pipes; two gold chains, about 45cm (18in) and 50cm (20in) long; two flat loops; a jump ring; a clasp (possibly also ball caps to hold the ends of the chains together securely); two feeder loops.

Method (see picture on page 12)   First of all, if necessary, bore a hole in the tip of the mother-of-pearl shape. The back of the mother-of-pearl needs to be rubbed down with sandpaper so that the glue adheres properly. The two feeder loops are each bent upwards on one side and are then pushed on to the bent pipes. Next, attach the jump ring to the teardrop pearl. After you have threaded the chain through the bent pipes and the jump ring, stick the feeder loops with the bent-up section on to the back of the mother-of-pearl. Stick the flat loops into position and pass the second chain through them. You can then attach the four chain-ends to the clasp.

FEATHER BROOCH (see page 11 – far left)

Materials One mother-of-pearl shape; one small bent pipe; three pieces of gold chain, each 16cm (6½ in) long; three feathers; four small beads; white modelling clay; one brooch-pin with a flat head.

Method Thread the three lengths of chain through the bent pipe. Position the bent pipe as required and attach using modelling clay. Take care that the brooch does not become too thick. Harden in the oven and allow to cool. Then separate the pieces (modelling clay, bent pipe, and mother-of-pearl) and stick them together again, using glue, so that they will stand up to more wear. As soon as the glue has dried sufficiently, stick the feathers in place (two of which will have the beads threaded on to them) and the brooch-pin.

PEARL BROOCH (see page 11 – left)

Materials One mother-of-pearl shape; a small bent pipe; three pieces of gold chain, each 14cm (5½in) long; one pearl teardrop (small); one jump ring; white oven-bakeable modelling clay; one brooch-pin with a flat head.

Method Assemble this brooch in the same way as the previous brooch, with the exception of the feathers. Before hardening the mother-of-pearl you will need to bore a hole in it through which to hang the pearl teardrop.

EARRINGS (see page 11 – far right)

Materials Two teardrop pearls (large); two jump rings; two small bent pipes (same diameter as chain); two earring attachments; two pieces of gold chain, each 12cm (4¾in) long.

Method When buying the chain, make sure that the individual links are sufficiently large to hang the various items from. Hang a teardrop pearl from the middle of each length of chain. Then thread both lengths of chain through the bent pipes and secure

the two ends using a jump ring. Once the earring attachments are in place, the earrings are ready to wear.

Discreet jewellery

NECKLACE (see page 13 – right)

Materials Five mother-of-pearl shapes; five flat loops; five small lentil-shaped beads; ten small bent pipes (short); one spring clasp (possibly also two ball caps to hold the chain-ends securely in place); one chain of the required length.

Method Lightly sand the spots where the glue is to be applied and glue flat loops to the back of the mother-of-pearl. These should be left to dry for at least five hours.

The individual pieces are then threaded in the appropriate order on to the chain, as shown in the picture on page 13. The links in this chain are sufficiently large to allow attachment of the clasp without using ball caps. When buying a chain, however, always check the strength of the links.

CHOKER AND EARRINGS (see above – left)

Materials Three mother-of-pearl shapes; two long bent pipes; eight short bent pipes (twisted); eight small lentil-shaped beads; one choker; one flat loop; two earring attachments (with clip-on mechanism); two jump rings.

Method First of all, lightly sand one of the mother-of-pearl shapes in the places where the glue is to be applied. Stick the flat loop in place and leave it to dry for at least five hours to allow the glue to set properly.

Then unscrew the ball from the choker and thread the individual pieces on to it in the right order (see picture above). Finally, screw the ball on again tightly. The selection and ordering of the metal pieces can be varied to suit your taste. For the earrings, take care not to bore the holes too close to the edge of the mother-of-pearl. Fix the earring attachments to the mother-of-pearl using the jump rings, which are then closed using two pairs of pliers.

13

Mother-of-pearl and freshwater pearls

NECKLACE (see below – left)

Materials Four closed strands of freshwater pearls (one violet, one light blue, two pink; each 90cm (36in) long); four pieces of mother-of-pearl (of equal size); six jump rings; two large snap hooks; one small snap hook.

Method First of all, bore a hole in the mother-of-pearl shapes. Using the jump rings, position the mother-of-pearl shapes at the required distance from one another along one of the strings of beads (e.g. the light-blue one). Arrange the four strings of pearls to form a broad necklace with the mother-of-pearl suspended in the middle. Then attach a large snap hook to each end of the strings of pearls. The large snap hooks are linked to the small one with two jump rings to form the clasp (see diagram below). There

are many variations possible for this necklace, using any number of strands of pearls.

NECKLACE (see page 14 – right)

Materials One large piece of mother-of-pearl with two holes in it; three round strands of freshwater pearls (pink, green, and violet); one round clasp.

Method For this necklace you can use the natural holes in the mother-of-pearl and thread the three strands of pearls (which have been twisted together) through these holes. Then attach the clasp.

Mother-of-pearl with masks

BROOCHES (see below – left and far right)

Materials Various mother-of-pearl shapes; small masks; brooch-pins.

Method Lightly sand the back of the mother-of-pearl shapes. Then stick the masks on to the front of the tips of the shapes. (When buying the masks, make sure that they fit as exactly as possible on to the tips of the mother-of-pearl). The brooches can be further

decorated, as required, with small chains which are glued in place. When the glue has set, stick a brooch-pin on to the back.

CHOKER (see page 15 – right)

Materials Two mother-of-pearl shapes; two small masks; four diamanté rondelles; one pendant with fringe; four small bent pipes; one metal choker; one jump ring; white modelling clay.

Method Stick the masks on to the mother-of-pearl, and allow the glue to set firmly before continuing. Unscrew the ball from the choker. Thread on a small bent pipe, a diamanté rondelle, and then another tube. Next, attach the first piece of mother-of-pearl to the choker using modelling clay, keeping the centre of the choker in mind. The choker should be completely covered by clay. Next, attach a diamanté rondelle, then the fringe using a jump ring (this should be flexible) and, finally, another rondelle. Then attach the second piece of mother-of-pearl, again using modelling clay. The remaining bent pipes and the diamanté rondelle can be carefully threaded on to the choker and the tiny ball screwed on again. The finished article should then be laid carefully in the oven to harden. Remove the mother-of-pearl once more and attach it using glue – the jewellery will last longer if you do.

HAIR-SLIDE (see page 15 – top)

Materials Two mother-of-pearl shapes; one mask (large); one hair-slide attachment; white modelling clay.

Method Spread the white modelling clay on to the hair-slide in such a way that both pieces of mother-of-pearl, with the mask between them, can be placed in position. Use plenty of modelling clay, as it needs to fill out the natural contours of the mother-of-pearl. After the hair-slide has been hardened and has cooled down again, carefully separate the slide, the mother-of-pearl, and the mask, and stick them all together again.

Eye-catching brooches

SQUARE BROOCHES (see page 17 – left)

Materials Mother-of-pearl shapes; modelling clay (black); jewels (iridescent); brooch-pins (with flat heads); gold powder.

Method For these brooches the decorative extras are modelled in clay. Before dusting them with powdered gold, press them firmly into place on the mother-of-pearl so that they stick well. It is best, however, to remove the pieces made from modelling clay carefully after hardening and attach them once again with glue. Stick the jewels and the brooch-pin on after hardening.

BROOCHES WITH CHAINS (see page 17 – right and centre)

Materials Mother-of-pearl shapes; jewels; brooch-pins; florist's wire (thin).

Method Firstly, assemble the chains as in the diagram on page 17, using 3cm (1¼in) pieces of wire. Make sure that the distances between the loops of chain are equal. When the loops are all in place, twist the U-shaped wire-ends with a pair of pliers so that the chain does not slip. Then, line the back of the mother-of-pearl with a layer of white modelling clay 3–4mm (⅛–³⁄₁₆in) thick. Press the pieces of wire holding the chain in place into the modelling clay: make sure that the wire is completely covered with the clay. After

hardening, carefully remove the clay from the mother-of-pearl and stick it back in place. As soon as the glue has set, you can stick the jewels on to the front and the brooch-pin on to the back. Allow to set once again.

Assembling the hanging chains for the brooch at the centre (above).

Cords and abalone

Materials Three abalone shapes; one mother-of pearl shape; twenty-four thin cords 45cm (18in) long; four tulip-shaped end caps with pins; two clasps; four flat loops (large); two blanks for clip-on earrings.

Method Sand the backs of the shapes. For the earrings, simply stick clips on to the back – they are finished. For the necklaces, stick two flat loops on to the back of each abalone shape. Wind a piece of wire around the ends of the cords. Apply a drop of glue so that the pin stays securely in place. Place the tulip-shaped end cap over the point of the pin, then bend the pin with a pair of pliers to interlink with a loop to which the clasp is attached. Before placing the tulip-shaped end cap over the other ends of the cords, thread the cords through the flat loop attached to the pendant. Do not try your necklaces on until all the glue is completely dry.

Mother-of-pearl brooches with red tones

Materials Pieces of mother-of-pearl; brooch-blanks; black modelling clay; bronze powder (silver, red); matt varnish for modelling clay.

Method After you have filled the brooch-blanks with modelling clay, you can produce the various pieces using netting and a toothbrush. Press the mother-of-pearl into the position required in the arrangement. The remaining pieces in the arrangement, such as threads, small folds, and triangles, are modelled in clay and pressed into position. Make sure that the arrangement achieves a sense of balance. You can then apply the bronze powder. The strong red colour can be toned down by mixing in silver powder before application. After hardening and cooling, detach the clay pieces from the brooch-blank and stick them back in place. Finally, varnish the clay pieces: the fine patina of bronze powder adheres particularly well after varnishing.

Brooches and hair-slides

HAIR-SLIDES (see above – left)

Materials Two hair-slide attachments; transparent modelling clay; two large matching pieces of mother-of-pearl for each slide; one matching disc of mother-of-pearl for each slide; jewels.

Method Using transparent modelling clay, attach the pieces of mother-of-pearl to the hair-slide attachments in the shape of bows. The modelling clay is used here to fill out the natural contours of the mother-of-pearl. After hardening, carefully detach the pieces and then stick all them together again. Do make sure that the glue has set properly before you wear the hair slides.

BROOCH WITH DIAMANTÉ (see above – bottom right)

Materials One piece of mother-of-pearl of the required shape; four diamanté stones; one brooch-pin.

Method For this brooch, the diamanté stones were stuck into openings in the shell to conceal their backs. If you like, you can use a piece of mother-of-pearl without holes, but if you do, make sure that you only use flat-backed diamanté stones, because they stick to the surface of the mother-of-pearl better. As soon as the stones are securely in position you can stick the brooch-pin on to the back (sand the back lightly beforehand).

BROOCH IN THREE PARTS (see page 20 – top right)

Materials Three pieces of mother-of-pearl; one brooch-pin.

Method Simply stick the three pieces of mother-of-pearl together. You can attach the brooch-pin to the back as soon as the glue has dried on the three lightly sanded areas.

Square shapes

NECKLACE (see above – left)

Materials Twelve square pieces of mother-of-pearl; twenty-four jump rings; eleven silver beads; silver wire (0.6mm in diameter and about 50cm (20in) long); one spring clip.

Method Bore two holes in each piece of mother-of-pearl. Thread each bead on to a piece of silver wire

2cm (¾in) long and bend both ends of the wire into small loops. It is best to use a pair of round-nosed pliers for this. Attach a jump ring to each piece of mother-of-pearl and attach these to wire loops coming from the beads. The necklace is quite flexible and sits well around the neck. Finally, attach the clasp.

BROOCH (see page 21 – top left)

Materials One large square piece of mother-of-pearl; one small square piece of mother-of-pearl; one silver bead; silver wire (0.6mm in diameter, about 2cm (¾in) long); two jump rings; one brooch-pin.

Method Bore a hole in both pieces of mother-of-pearl. Thread the silver bead on to the wire and bend the ends of the wires into loops. Using jump rings, attach the mother-of-pearl and the bead to the wire. All you then need to do is stick the brooch-pin on to the back.

DROP EARRINGS (see page 21 – right)

Materials Six square pieces of mother-of-pearl; four silver beads; silver wire (0.6mm in diameter, about 15cm (6in) long); ten jump rings; two ear-studs with loop and ball.

Method Bore a hole in two of the pieces of mother-of-pearl and two holes in each of the remaining four pieces. Assemble the mother-of-pearl and the silver beads as for the necklace and fasten them together using jump rings. Again using jump rings, attach the ear-studs to the mother-of-pearl.

EARRINGS (see page 21 – bottom)

Materials Two pieces of mother-of-pearl; two ear studs with loop and ball.

Method Simply glue the earring fittings to the back of the mother-of-pearl.

Costume jewellery

'Jewellery should decorate a woman, not make her appear wealthy. For this reason I have always liked wearing costume jewellery.' Coco Chanel once said this – how right she was! Attractive, colour-coordinating accessories both complement and accentuate a woman's fashionable appearance; they express her personality. It is not always easy to find a suitable piece of jewellery, though, so why not make your own brooch or necklace? Have a rummage in your jewellery box. Is there anything in there that you no longer wear? Simply take old pieces of jewellery to pieces, reassemble them in a different way, and fix them in place with the help of oven-bakeable modelling clay – you will have made something unique.

Why not visit a flea market, a gemstone fair, or a craft fair? You will find a wide range of pieces on offer. Let your imagination run riot: you will discover how enjoyable it is to produce attractive and original costume jewellery. This section is intended to awaken your enthusiasm with the suggestions and numerous useful tips it has to offer. You may discover a new creative side to yourself! Whether you have already practised this hobby or are coming to it for the first time, you should find you have a lot of fun – *and* successful results.

BASIC MATERIALS AND TECHNIQUES

Materials

Oven-bakeable modelling clay; jewellery blanks (with or without rims) for brooches, pendants, earrings (clip-on or for pierced ears), belt fasteners, and tie-pins; diamanté and semi-precious stones; precious stones and agates; glass stones and beads; fine glass tubes; pieces of mother-of-pearl; diamanté and artificial pearls of various sizes; decorative ornaments; embossed metal items; watch parts; gold and silver decorative chains (sold by the metre/yard); brass wire 0.4mm thick; sheet brass 0.5mm thick; cords; leather thongs and cotton laces; powder for decoration (gold, silver, copper, and blue); special varnish for oven-bakeable modelling clay (matt or gloss); epoxy adhesive; superglue; glue for ceramics.

Equipment

Tile or glass sheet; fine craft knife; glass bottle or plastic rolling pin; large darning needles; toothpick or awl; soft paintbrush (size 1 or 2); fabric; wire mesh; sandpaper; small sponge; an old pair of sharp-pointed nail scissors; two pairs of eyelet pliers; files; a very fine screwdriver.

Techniques

Oven-bakeable modelling clay comes in a wide range of colours and can be mixed to achieve different shades. Attractive shades (e.g. brown mixed with black, or blue with grey) provide a discreet background for your jewellery. The colours anthracite or brown, used in conjunction with pearly lustre, give a particularly fine gleaming finish. Dark colours have the advantage of giving a warmer appearance and an antique effect to silver and gold powder applied later on in the process.

Kneading Before you start, knead the modelling clay until it is pliable. Insufficient kneading may give you unattractive air bubbles during the hardening process which cannot be eliminated. Modelling material which has become very soft can be placed in the fridge for a short period. This will make it easier to handle.

Modelling Under the piece of jewellery you are working on, place a piece of modelling clay, and then press them both down on to the work-tile. This will stop the piece slipping whilst you are modelling.

Attaching Pieces of modelling clay stick to one another if you press them lightly together. Other materials, though, such as chains, metal shapes, stones, diamanté, and pearls, need to be secured in place using epoxy adhesive; otherwise they could come away from the modelling clay later on whilst being worn. Try to be precise with the glue, because it can leave dull whitish marks on the surface of the jewellery if you get it in the wrong place, or if it squeezes out from underneath something.

Hardening Your pieces of jewellery need to be hardened in the oven for a minimum of twenty to thirty minutes. The correct temperature for an electric oven is 100° to 130° C (210° to 260°), for a fan-assisted oven 80° to 100°C (180° to 210°F), and for a gas oven the very lowest setting. Note that some colours of clay need to be hardened at the *lowest* temperature: always check the manufacturers' instructions. Keep an eye on light-coloured clay to make sure it does not darken or turn brown. (Laying a piece of tinfoil over the item of jewellery will protect it against excessive heat). Afterwards leave the pieces in the oven until they have cooled down completely.

Varnishing After the hardening process, apply the special varnish gently and sparingly to the modelled decorative feature using a paintbrush. This fixes the bronze powder. Several coats of sparingly applied varnish on top will stop the metallic effect rubbing off. Using a paintbrush you can also apply an emulsion of bronze powder mixed with varnish. In this way you can vary or intensify shades of colour.

Filling in a jewellery blank Roll out a piece of modelling clay on the work-tile, apply glue to the jewellery blank, and spread it out lightly using a paper tissue. Place the rolled-out modelling clay in the frame and smooth it out to the edges with your thumb, cutting away any excess clay with a knife. You might like to

Filling in a jewellery blank

use fabric (netting or lace) or other substances (wire mesh, or various metal objects) to texturize the item.

Texturizing the clay

Inlaying chains If you are using stones, position those first and glue them in place. For chains which are only intended to be decorative, first of all score a line in the modelling clay with a needle. Apply ceramic glue to the point of the needle and apply to the first 1 or 2cm (½–¾in) of the scored line. Position the chain and press gently: continue in this way until you

Inlaying chains

reach the end of the chain. Using nail scissors, carefully cut through the chain and stick the end of the chain in place. The glue will soon dry and then you can press the chain more firmly into place. The glue will not spread, so the chain will be perfectly clean against its background. Cut any chains for hanging to the required length. Secure the ends of the chains firmly in place on the metal base of the brooch-blank using glue: in this instance use superglue. Place a small

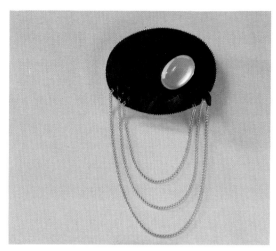

Hanging chains

disc of modelling clay over the point where the chain is attached to the brooch and work it in well to fill out the contours.

Decorative moulding Roll out a piece of modelling clay until it is about 3mm (⅛in) thick. Cut out a decorative feature (e.g. a leaf) to the desired size. Shape the leaf using a needle and your left thumb and forefinger. Keeping the leaf on the work-tile, apply bronze powder lightly or generously, according to the effect you want, using a paintbrush. Twist the modelling clay into small pointed shapes and notch them using the needle. Position small pieces of modelling clay on metal shapes (widely available in specialist shops) and mould gently; decorate the brooch with diamanté stones, pearls, and other accessories.

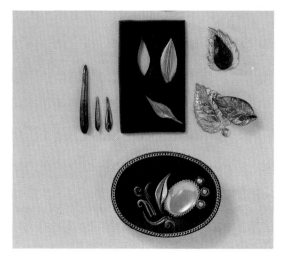

Decorative moulding

Fascination in black

Black stones have always been preferred to others in the production of costume jewellery. Whether onyx is used or cut-glass Tiffany stones, they are all distinctive, precious, and very attractive.

Materials Brooch-blanks in four different shapes; two earring attachments; two hooks; black stones; figaro chains; trace chains; decorative trace chains; beads; small glass tubes or bugle beads; diamanté stones.

Method To make these five items of jewellery, follow the general instructions given on pages 24–5.

Gentlemen's jewellery

Tie- and lapel-pins are fashionable for women as well as for men.

Transparent stones, and long ones, go well with the narrow fittings. A few discreet decorative features made from modelling clay enhance the angular shapes of the jewellery. These delicate pins should not be overwhelmed by excessive decoration.

Materials Two lapel-pins with oval fittings; four different tie-clip attachments; a square brooch-blank; an elongated grey jewel (imitation); two white mirror-backed glass stones; a flat, square piece of onyx; a multicoloured, long, flat piece of glass; grey enamelled glass tubes; dark-grey and golden beads; trace chains;

figaro chains; decorative chains; diamanté stones; different-sized beads.

Method Position the enamelled tubes on the modelling clay in the tie-pin (bottom centre of picture) and on the brooch which is similar in design (bottom left of picture). Press them into the surface and then remove them. Carefully apply a little glue into the impressions you have made, using the point of a needle, and put the tubes back in their original positions. Wait a moment before pressing, so that the glue does not squeeze out from under the sides. Fill in the gaps between the glass tubes with golden and grey beads.

Treasures from the sea

How about creating a completely personal item of jewellery using a souvenir from your last seaside holiday? On the beach you can find all sorts of shells, sometimes with natural holes in them.

Materials One large, round mother-of-pearl shape; one pink shell; one half of a mother-of-pearl shell; beige-coloured cord; two cord attachments; an anchor chain; a silvery decorative chain; three catches; oval beads; round beads; golden beads; different-sized diamanté stones.

Method In order to achieve an attractive effect, the flat, round mother-of-pearl shape requires a large design feature, whereas a smaller shell requires more delicate decoration. Fasten the cord and chain ends to the back of the shell using superglue. The back will look nice and neat if you stick a thin layer of modelling clay to it and harden the clay.

Tip 'Foreign material' does not stick to the chalky surface of the shell very well, so glue everything thoroughly and press the two surfaces firmly together.

A dream in pink

Amongst the wide range of polished stones available you are sure to find your favourite colour. Do you like light blue, green, or perhaps a warm marbled pink?

Materials Two oval-shaped portrait-format brooch-blanks; an oval brooch-blank with chain rings; two round blanks for clip-on earrings; a cabochon with a painting on it; a pink, square stone; three oval stones with pink marbling; trace chains; figaro chains; decorative chains; twisted brass wire; melon beads; round beads; gold-coloured beads and diamanté stones.

Semi-precious stones such as tiger's-eye, agates or rose quartz are inexpensive to buy in craft shops, at a gemstone fair, or in specialist shops for Tiffany requisites. At flea markets and craft fairs you can often find charming miniatures painted on porcelain, and grandmother's jewellery box is another good place to look.

Method For the rose brooch, the porcelain should look dainty, rather like an antique heirloom. To tone in with the rose, the narrow edge which you have modelled in clay can be tinted using pink eye-shadow.

Summer necklaces

You could easily develop some highly original forms for your costume jewellery: what about something to go with a particular garment?

Materials Five oval blanks for drop earrings; a large metal ring; two hooks; two ear studs; sheet brass 0.5mm thick; brass wire; five long black stones; a faceted glass stone; sixteen large diamanté stones for insetting; black glass tubes; gold, silver, and black beads of varying sizes; small diamanté stones; trace chains with two catches.

Method Follow the general techniques on pages 24–5. For the very original pendant (bottom right in the picture above), join three teardrop-shaped earring blanks together. Apply epoxy adhesive to the joins, fix it in the oven, and fasten the three parts together with a large metal ring.

Both pendants have home-made bases (see the templates below). Lay a cardboard template on a sheet of brass 0.5mm thick, trace the outline using a sharp object, and cut out using a strong pair of scissors. File down cut edges and corners with a fine metal file. Attach the metal rings using epoxy adhesive. Stick a piece of rolled-out modelling clay on to the metal and spread out to the sides until the surface is thinly coated. Remove any excess from the edges using a knife. Use netting or sandpaper to give the surface texture and edge the piece with chains before adding any further embellishments (see page 25). Position spacers such as black glass tubes and gold and silver beads threaded on to brass wire evenly along the trace chains. They tone with the stone in colour and in shape and look really lovely.

The matching earrings to both sets are made in the same way.

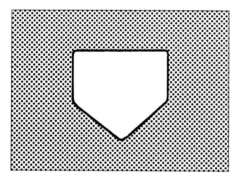

Template for pendant on page 30 (top centre) – actual size.

Template for pendant on page 30 (bottom centre) – actual size.

Stylish elegance

White stones incorporated into jewellery have a very discreet and elegant effect when their brightness is echoed by a piece of silver chain or a pearly decoration.

Materials Various brooch-blanks; a round piece of mother-of-pearl; a triangular piece of mother-of-pearl; a glass stone with mother-of-pearl finish; a brass ornament incorporating a small moonstone; two white mirror-backed stones; gold and silver trace chains; figaro chain; beads; diamanté stones; glass stones.

Method These brooches are made using the techniques on pages 24–5. An unusual feature is the round piece of mother-of-pearl in the semicircular pin. As it protrudes above the brooch-base, it needs to be secured firmly to the surface of the modelling clay using epoxy adhesive. Be careful not to use superglue to stick the mirror-backed stones in place: the mirrored backing would come off after the hardening process and the stone would lose its shine and darken. Use only porcelain adhesive or glue designed specifically for ceramics.

31

Watch-part jewellery

The really good thing about this kind of jewellery is that you can be as imaginative as you like when moving the bits and pieces around. As with a collage, you will discover various central motifs which you can then echo in smaller or different forms.

Materials Various brooch-blanks and watch parts; gilt trace chains; silver rope chains; gold beads; black glass tubes; diamanté stones.

Method Using very fine screwdrivers, dismantle old, defunct watches, or buy the parts in a craft shop. Experiment with different combinations of watch parts and other items of jewellery, then prepare the bases and chains with modelling clay. When you are completely satisfied with the arrangement, glue the pieces into position, remembering to use the glue sparingly. If the watch parts overlap, use modelling clay to pad out the uneven surface and blend that clay carefully into the background clay.

Pearls and mother-of-pearl

Artificial pearls are big news. Teardrops, olive-shaped pearls or the more common round pearls can all be used to make elegant costume jewellery.

Materials Three different-sized brooch-blanks; two brass rings with ear-wires; a semicircular piece of mother-of-pearl; an oval mother-of-pearl stone; a triangular piece of mother-of-pearl; a metal decoration incorporating a white stone; three imitation pearl teardrops with chased bell cap; trace chains; figaro chains; cord chains; pearls and diamanté stones in various sizes.

Method For the hoop earrings, coat the brass rings on both sides with modelling clay and then harden in the oven. Next, decorate the front, harden, and then complete the back with the same pattern. Attach the pearl teardrop. For the semicircular and oval brooches, due to the uneven surface of the back of the mother-of-pearl, apply modelling material liberally to the base and press the mother-of-pearl firmly into place to avoid any hollow spaces. Use decorative silver chains and small rows of pearls for the border; they bring out the shimmering qualities of the mother-of-pearl.

An expedition to the gemstone fair

You can find lots of lovely jewellery elements at a gemstone fair. Slices of agate, with their varied forms and shades, can be converted into brooches by the addition of a brooch-bar.

Materials A square brooch-blank; a brown ribbon agate; a slice of agate; two ammonites; brooch-bars; a brass anchor-chain with a catch; a small mask; feathers; diamanté stones and pearls in various shapes and sizes.

Method Before decorating the brooches, attach the brooch-bars using epoxy adhesive. If the metal part is visible through the brooch, then conceal with decoration on the front.

The twin ammonites need to be embedded in black modelling clay to hold them together. Now decorate this unique pendant with pearls and diamanté stones, attach the anchor chain to the back using superglue, and wipe it clean using a strip of leather.

Prepare the mask brooch in three stages. First of all, press a small ball of modelling clay into a mask-shaped mould which you have lightly dusted with gold powder (to make it easier to remove) and carefully remove it again. Model the features using the head of a pin and harden it for the first time. Roll another ball of modelling clay, make a hat from it, stick the hat on to the head, and harden it for a second time. Arrange feathers on the completed mask and

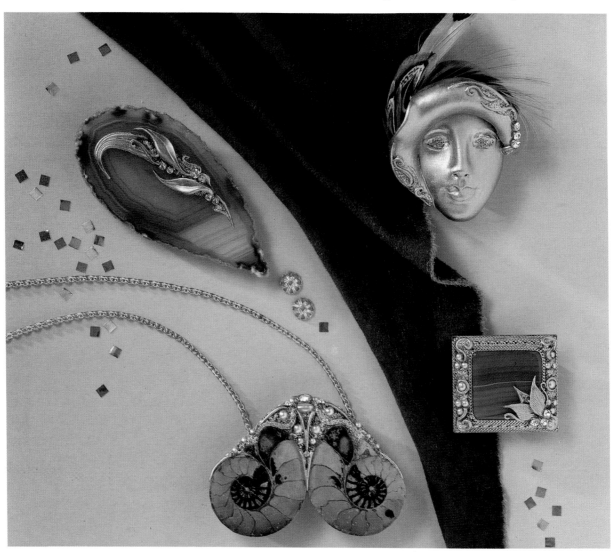

stick them in place. Use modelling clay to model decorative elements, stick them neatly on to the hat, and harden for a third time. Use varnish to fix the gold and silver powders. Attach the brooch-bar using epoxy adhesive.

Variations in copper, gold, and blue

Copper, gold, and blue – what a wonderful combination of colours for unusual costume jewellery!

Materials An oval brooch-blank; two pairs of blanks for clip-on earrings (round and oval); trace chains; figaro chains; three chain fasteners; oval, round, and olive-shaped pearls; diamanté stones and gold beads; blue, gold, and coppery-red metallic powder.

Method The three pendants are formed straight on to a work-tile without a metal back. As the procedures for all these necklaces are similar, only the procedure for making the semicircular pendant is explained below.

Roll out a piece of modelling clay on the work-tile until it is 3mm (1/8in) thick, cut out the required shape, and smooth down the edges with a finger. Then rub in some copper metallic powder, trace a line with the needle for the chain the pendant is to hang from, and stick the chain in place. Where the chain joins the pendant, strengthen the bond at both points with superglue.

Cut out a long strip of modelling material, form it into a semicircle, colour it using blue metallic powder

and stick it gently in place covering the chain. Use the darning needle to dot or roughen the surface of the inner semicircle and then apply gold powder with a paintbrush. Model decorative features from modelling clay, colour them separately on the work-tile using gold, and then stick them into position. Decorate the individual pieces with diamanté stones or pearls and place the finished items, still on the work-tile, into the oven to harden. After cooling, remove the finished pendants from the tile using a sharp knife. Fix the metallic powder with varnish.

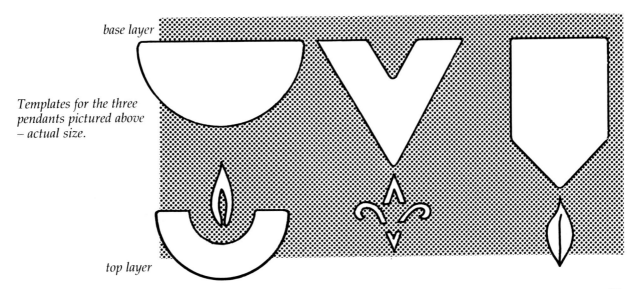

base layer

Templates for the three pendants pictured above – actual size.

top layer

Mix and match

Would you like to make some drop earrings to match a necklace or brooch you already possess? Stones similar in type and colour, with jewellery designs to match, really enhance the effect of the ensemble.

Materials One square brooch-blank; one octagonal brooch-blank; three sorts of earring blanks in various shapes; two shepherd's-crook ear-wires; four clip-on earring attachments; sheet brass; two pendant rings; an anchor chain with a catch; three black stones; three glass teardrops decorated with gold threads; three tortoiseshell-patterned glass rectangles; eight large diamanté stones in metal settings; trace chains; figaro chains; fluted metal beads; black glass tubes; small diamanté stones; silver beads.

Method For the octagonal set apply a little gold powder underneath the tortoiseshell-patterned glass. It shines through the glass in the more transparent places, really bringing it to life.

Form the gold and silver triangular pendant on a tile and strengthen it from behind using an appropriately sized piece of sheet brass (see template on page 38). Arrange laces of golden modelling material over the pendant from bottom to top in a chess-board pattern. Leaving the individual chambers smooth, dot the outer track and the triangle above with a needle and dust with silver powder. Finish off with large and small diamanté stones. For the rest of the jewellery, follow the general instructions on pages 24–5.

Jewellery for the ball

A large belt fastener like this is attractive and yet easy to make.

Materials A belt base with 4cm (1½in) belt carriers; black elasticated band 4cm (1½in) wide; two earring blanks with ear-wires attached; sheet brass; two chain rings; a large black round glass stone; a gold-coloured metal ornament; four square black stones; trace chains; rope chains; a black leather thong; 40cm (16in) of black cord with four cord-holders and a catch; beads and diamanté stones of various sizes.

Method For the belt fastener, frame the dark round glass stone with the chains and the black leather thong. The gold-coloured metal ornament is an additional feature. Bend the ornament to correspond to the shape of the stone and carefully stick in place. Follow the basic guidelines given on pages 24–5 as well as the instructions for pendants on pages 35–6 and the diagram below when making the distinctive ballroom-jewellery ensemble. Cut the small hanging chains to be exactly symmetrical only after the hardening process.

Template for pendant (top left) on page 37 – actual size.

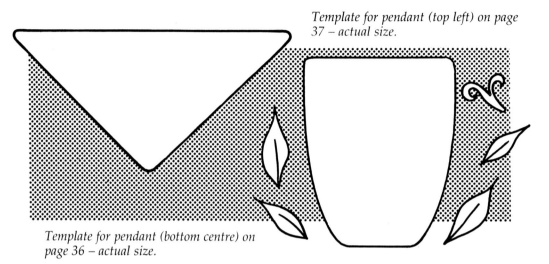

Template for pendant (bottom centre) on page 36 – actual size.

Fashion jewellery

Have you ever lost the right necklace for your new dress, or found that the jewellery you have simply does not suit your clothes? Well, now you can change all that. In minutes you can create an item of jewellery for your ear, wrist, or neck which not only suits you but also tones perfectly with your clothing. Once you have tapped your latent talent your creative imagination will know no bounds. Nowadays you can buy such a wide variety of jewellery components that you will get great pleasure from designing your own personal jewellery:
the possibilities are endless.
Moreover, the ideas in this section could also serve as an inspiration for male jewellery designers looking for an original idea for a present! A bit of courage is all you really need – the rest is child's play.

6

BASIC MATERIALS AND TECHNIQUES

Materials

A variety of metal beads and spacers; coloured beads of various shapes and sizes, likewise beads with a shiny metal finish; ceramic beads of various shapes and colours; variously shaped jewellery elements in different colours with a shiny metal finish; small bent pipes; dividing and gripping elements in various shapes and sizes; round leather thongs, round cotton laces, and satin laces of various thicknesses and colours; cords in rayon, viscose, and cotton of various thicknesses and colours; chokers in two sizes; brass and silver wire; spring catches for thongs; closure caps with rings in various shapes and sizes; connecting rings and dividing rings; screw catches and snap hooks; earring attachments (clip-ons and for pierced ears).

Equipment

A pair of round-nosed pliers; a pair of small flat-nosed pliers with side cutter; scissors; adhesive tape; strong, fine thread; multi-purpose glue; a pair of tweezers.

Techniques

All the pieces of jewellery presented in this section are very easy to copy. They are only intended to provide a stimulus, though – your own personal taste and your individual style of dress will demand your own creations. Feel free to change any of these suggestions: lengthen or shorten necklaces; choose different colours; select your favourite shapes from amongst the wide range of individual findings on offer; improvise by replacing unavailable materials

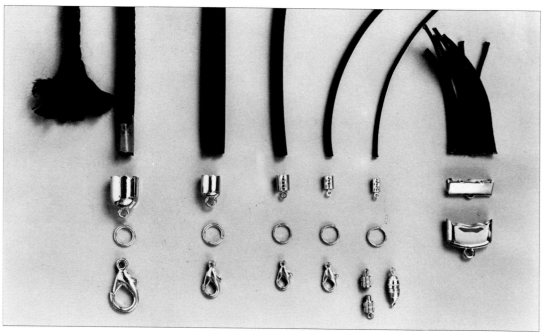

A selection of thongs and laces, closure caps, jump rings, and catches.

with other ones. The game of fantasy begins at the buying stage, where you have the whole range of chokers, laces, and individual elements laid out before you.

As making fashion jewellery is very simple and the tasks are repetitive, only a few tips are outlined here. For a necklace the laces or thongs should be between 40cm (16in) and 60cm (24in) in length and for bracelets between 18cm (7¼in) and 24cm (9½in). The easiest method of making jewellery is by threading together different jewellery elements. It is possible, however, to attach clip-on jewellery elements to a bundle of thongs (you can see several kinds in the picture on page 45). Please remember, though, that catches will lengthen the piece of jewellery by a few centimetres (half an inch or so). If a necklace should turn out to be too short you can lengthen it by inserting small chains (sold by the metre/yard) between the rings. Note that the metal parts will not lose their gleam, as they have been gold-plated or nickel-plated.

Attaching catches There are grip catches and tulip-shaped end caps of various sizes; there are twist-off catches and snap hooks, and nickel-plated and gold-plated bolt rings. The grip catches are open on one side. If you need to bring together several thongs in a tulip-shaped end cap, bind them together using strong thread, apply strong glue, and press them into the tulip-shaped end cap. The bonding strength of glues available nowadays is surprisingly good. A snap hook, combined with two rings, will lengthen a necklace by 3cm (1¼in).

Threading parts together To facilitate threading the various elements together, wrap sticky tape tightly around the thread or threads and cut off at an angle. Individual elements with very small holes can then be threaded together by holding the taped end between the thumb and forefinger and pushing it through the hole, twisting it as it goes.

INDIVIDUAL PIECES

Beads and teardrops

The picture above shows you that this jewellery can literally be made at the very last moment before wearing, provided that you have a minimum of material available.

Materials See the general list on page 40.

Method For the choker on the right you can start by simply threading on a ceramic bead in your favourite colour as a centre-piece. Thread on the other elements as in the picture. For the earrings (top right) you need two 10cm (4in) lengths of brass wire on which to thread the individual beads. Put the two ends together and twist a few times around the earring attachments to secure.

The choker on the left is a very simple one: you can vary the different parts as your fancy takes you.

Simple chokers and laces

Materials See the general list on page 40.

Method The simplest and quickest way to make your own jewellery is by threading the beads or elements on to a choker or a lace. Use a metal choker for the model on the left of the picture: unscrew the end bead and thread on alternately twenty-eight round gold beads and twenty-seven flat black beads.

As you can see from the picture, the choker in the middle has a centre-piece comprising six flat black ceramic discs, five metal spacers, and a black bead either side. Place a split ring between each bead and ceramic disc and insert an 8cm (3¼in) length of gold chain (sold by the metre/yard). On either side of the centre-piece there are two bent pipes with a black bead placed between and above them.

For the necklace at the bottom of the picture, take a cotton lace about 90cm (36in) in length and thread on alternately fourteen metal spacers and thirteen flat black ceramic discs. Working outwards on each side, thread on a further twelve golden beads and four black ones. These are then secured on either side by a knot. To wear the necklace, tie the ends of the lace together.

For the earrings, cut an 8cm (3¼in) length of cotton lace and thread the different beads on to it. Press both ends of the lace into the grip catch and attach to the ear-wires.

Jewellery in green

Materials See the general list on page 40.

Method For the necklace on the left of the picture you need four cotton laces, each about 50cm (20in) in length. Thread the four laces through all the different findings except the small ceramic bead. Thread only the two inner laces through the small bead, bringing the two outer ones over the bead. Once past the large bead and the golden ring, thread the two inner laces through the two golden rings, divide the laces, and thread each pair through the bent pipes. Attach the

clasp as described on page 41. Knot a small metal bead at the bottom of each lace. For the necklace on the right of the picture you need eleven laces, each approx 50cm (20in) in length. Thread a few metal shells on to a few laces at a time. Now feed all the laces through the first tube. Arrange the loops so that they hang as shown in the picture and feed them through the second tube. Gather the laces together, with an eye to the shortest one, and attach the fastener with glue.

44

Leather thong necklaces

Materials See the general list on page 40.

Method For the necklace at the top of the picture, feed five leather thongs each about 50cm (20in) long through the gripping elements, attaching a metal shell between each one. Attach four gold beads centrally at the front. Working out from the centre to the two ends, arrange the thongs by hand to achieve a rounded form, until you are happy with the effect. Now all you have to do is attach the fastener.

The necklace on the left of the picture consists of twenty leather thongs. The lattice effect is produced by feeding alternately four then five thongs through the metal shells. Lay the necklace on the table and arrange it to suit your taste. On either side slip on a few more metal shells over the leather thongs. For the fastener, gather the thongs together, again with an eye to the shortest one.

For the decorative chain, bottom right, measure out ten leather thongs each approx 50cm (20in) long (the leather sometimes varies in thickness). Thread all the thongs but one through the spacer bars and arrange the spacer bars as you like. Finally, thread the outer leather thong through, threading on beads and tubes between the spacer bars. Necklace side bars with rings attached make a suitable catch.

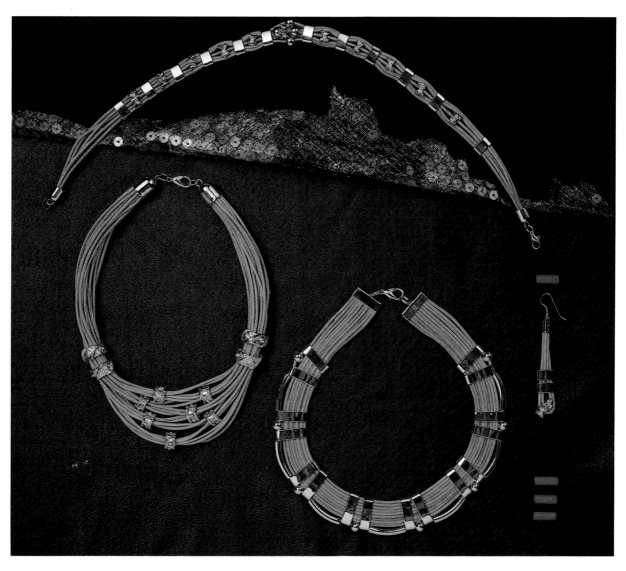

Decorative cord jewellery

Cord jewellery has a very gentle appearance and looks good when colour-coordinated to your clothing. It also accentuates your femininity.

Materials See the general list on page 40.

Method For the necklace at the top of the picture arrange the three lengths of cord in a circular pattern. The inner piece measures about 38cm (15¼in) and the outer piece about 43cm (17¼in). Thread on the double tubes as in the picture. Use a broad end cap for the clasp. To make it easier to insert the cords into the clasp, bind the ends tightly with sticky tape and square them off.

For the necklace at the bottom of the picture you need two thick, black cords each 45cm (18in) in length. Fold both cords in two and bind the ends with sticky tape. You will then have two pieces of cord, each 22cm (8¾in) in length. On the opposite side, thread a metal shell with a large hole on to the cord and fit a bail on the other cord. By fitting a ring you will prevent the bails from slipping out of position. (This is the point at which you can alter the length of the necklace.) Finally, attach the clasp.

The earrings are made along the same lines.

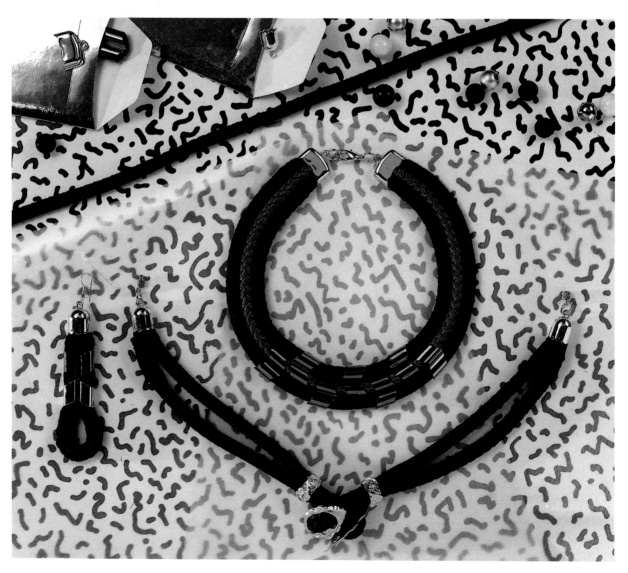

Modelled clay jewellery

Most of the jewellery presented in this section has resulted from experimenting with metal elements and modelling clay. Using coloured modelling clay in combination with gold- and silver-coloured elements enables you to follow the fashionable colours of the moment. The modelling clay is so easy to use and there is such a variety of materials and accessories that you can really get your own ideas and creativity going, whether you are having to work quickly or taking your time over a creation. You can produce pieces which are elegant or casual, ostentatious or discreet, giving you a wide range of attractive jewellery from which to choose, with something to suit every occasion. These pages will inspire you to make original jewellery using new techniques and guide you towards your own successful and enjoyable work.

BASIC MATERIALS AND TECHNIQUES

Materials

Oven-bakeable modelling clay; pieces of mother-of-pearl; glass stones and semi-precious stones; precious stones (possibly!); different-sized beads; artificial pearls; decorative chains; cords; leather thongs (natural or coloured); gold balls; metal beads; belts, leather or elasticated; pendant-mounting chokers with unscrewable ends; metal leaves for imprinting; metal masks and hands; fine paintbrushes; special varnish for oven-bakeable clay (not nitrocellulose or spray-on); gold and silver markers; mother-of-pearl buttons; blanks with smooth and milled edges for brooches, brooches with chains, bangles, pendants, tie-pins, bracelets, clip-on earrings, drop earrings, and belt fasteners; settings for diamanté; diamanté stones, sizes 1 to 5; diamanté or crystal stones, quality 1A, sizes 1 to 5 (available in craft shops as clear stones or in several colours) – the more valuable the stone, the better the cut and the more beautiful the resulting sparkle; decorative chains and trace chains (sold by the metre/yard); powder in bronze, silver, gold, antique gold, copper, pewter, green, grey, purple, and blue for decoration; matt varnish; epoxy adhesive; leather glue; crystal glue; eyeshadow.

Equipment

Kitchen knife; sheet of plate glass or ceramic tile as work-surface; rolling pin; tweezers; tooth-pick or metal skewer; cotton-wool buds or dowelling for modelling; toothbrush and sieve for texturizing; manicure set; brandy glass and cocktail glass; casserole dish about 30cm (12in) in diameter (see page 55); scissors; a pair of small pliers; tinfoil to make stencil; make-up brush, about 15mm (½in) wide; sharp scissors (old nail scissors).

Techniques

Oven-bakeable modelling clay is available in a wide variety of colours and in different-sized packets from specialist craft shops. For the items of jewellery in the picture, mainly black modelling clay has been used, because it shows the stones and bronze powder off to their best advantage. By using coloured modelling clay and by blending clays, however, you can also make fashionable brooches, pendants, belt

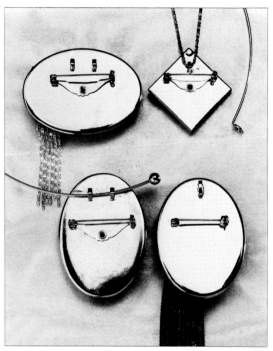

Combined chain brooches have rings on the back for attaching chokers or chains. The punched-out holes tend to get clogged up with clay, but you can gently unblock them with a toothpick before hardening.

fasteners or earrings. By mixing together two or more colours you can produce a marbled effect or a new shade of colour to tone with your wardrobe. Try mixing multicoloured left-overs together and see what amazing effects you can create!

Note that when you are producing large belts without a base component you should always prepare a template and cut out a shape in tinfoil or sheet copper.

Kneading To achieve the desired effects it is essential to knead the modelling clay thoroughly. Nothing could be uglier or more annoying than the sight of blisters which have arisen during the hardening of finished pieces due to insufficient kneading. Please take into account the following instructions. The softer and more pliable the clay has become through kneading, the easier and more successful it is to model with. Taking only small lumps of clay, knead them into balls and small rolls. Knead the lumps thoroughly with the palms of your hands until they are pliable. A good test is to cut the ball through the middle: there should be no 'crumbs' visible inside. For a larger piece of jewellery, for example a belt buckle, prepare as many balls and rolls as you need, lay them alongside each other, and roll them out together to the desired thickness. Do not expose modelling clay to heat or it may dry out or crumble (do not work near a heater). Resist the temptation to model clay on your patio in the sun! Once opened, packets are best stored in tins.

Attaching Use an epoxy adhesive to stick the modelling clay to the brooch-base. Spread equal quantities of glue over the modelling clay and the base component before pressing firmly together. If you are using several colours of clay, apply glue to them and position them one at a time. The glue can be fired in the oven as well. When insetting larger stones, cut a hole in the modelling clay down to the base, apply glue to the under-side of the stone, and fix the stone directly on to the base. Please read the instructions carefully for application of the glue.

Hardening The modelling clay then needs to be hardened: in an electric oven at 100° to 130°C (210° to 260°F), in a fan-assisted oven at 80° to 100°C (180° to 210°F), or in a gas oven on the lowest setting. Note that some colours of clay need to be hardened at the lowest temperature: always check manufacturers' instructions. (Test for temperature by hardening a sample beforehand.) Hardening takes about fifteen to twenty minutes.

To prevent any mishaps from occurring during the hardening process, take a look at the clay from time to time whilst it is in the oven, especially light-coloured clay, which might darken or turn brown. Allow hardened pieces to cool down to avoid crumbling or cracking.

There is now a small electric oven available on the market which has been specially designed to harden this synthetic modelling clay.

Any tarnishing of the metal parts which may occur as a result of heating can be removed by polishing with a cloth for cleaning silver or gold.

Varnishing After allowing the item to cool sufficiently, varnish it first thinly and then generously, using a special varnish for modelling clay (matt or gloss). If you are using any stones, clean them with a cotton-wool bud dipped in methylated spirit.

Filling in a jewellery blank Press a flat, semicircular piece of clay into the brooch-base and trim it with a knife. Then apply a second or third colour (see section on attaching, above). The next step is very important. To be sure that the brooch-base is evenly filled with modelling clay, use the knife to remove any protruding clay (not too fast or you might get a rough or cracked surface). Use the edge of the brooch as a guide to ensure an even finish. The layer you have just removed is the mirror image of the layer left behind and if it is sufficiently thick, you can make another brooch out of it, using it with the under-side facing up. In this way you have produced an almost identical counter-piece (this simplifies the construction of a set).

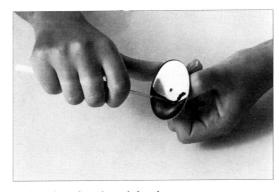

Trimming the edge of the clay

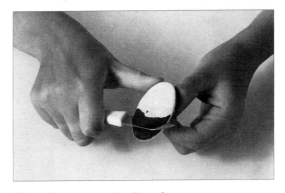

Removing any protruding clay

49

Inlaying chains When setting a chain in an oval base, start at the top edge in the centre. It is important to start with a complete link if you are using a decorative chain. Using your left thumb, press the chain into position parallel to the edge, feeding the chain between thumb and forefinger to avoid getting a twist in the chain. The more care and precision involved when setting the chain, the more exact your piece of jewellery will appear when it is finished. Moreover, it is not difficult to remove and reposition the chain correctly if you make a mistake. You do not always need to use glue to stick the chains into position on the modelling clay; if you press them into place well enough, you will probably find they will stick to the clay of their own accord, so run your thumb or forefinger several times over the chain. (For guidance on gluing chains, see page 25).

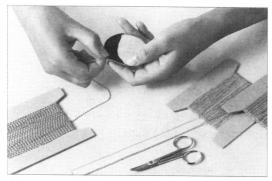

Inlaying a chain.

When you meet the other end of the chain, use a metal skewer to position the final section exactly and then, using a sharp pair of scissors, cut it off after a complete link. Press firmly into place and start working on the next chain.

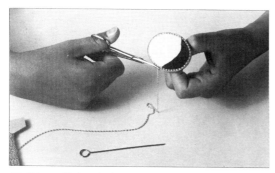

Cutting off the chain.

A particularly charming effect is achieved by inlaying first a decorative chain and then a trace chain beside it, and so on. You can proceed in this way, forming round or graphic patterns, as you wish. Dividing-lines between two or more colours can be marked by one or more chains.

Using decorative powders Now you can decorate the background with gold- or silver-coloured powder, according to the colour of the brooch-blank. Using a make-up brush about 15mm (1/2in) thick, dust the brooch lightly in certain areas, or cover it entirely with powder, or use a brush to coat the areas to neutralize bright colours. A marbled effect, which you can use all colours of powder to create, is achieved by applying the powder and rubbing it evenly in both directions using your index finger or middle finger. Only ever use the marbling technique on *white* modelling clay, however. Stick the clay in place using epoxy adhesive. Ensure that there are no traces of glue left on the finished jewellery, otherwise the powder will not adhere properly during the bronzing process and you will get unattractive matt patches.

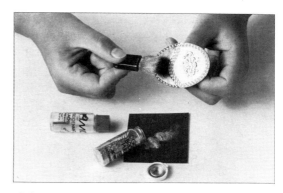

Colouring one section of the clay.

Tricolour technique For the tricolour technique, dust the surfaces of brooches or belt fasteners with different-coloured bronze powders or decorate them with leaves in different shades of bronze (see pages 56 and 60).   Stones or designs to be incorporated have to be firmly stuck in place on the clay base; the same goes for elements like diamanté and small beads.

Metal impressions By using metal shapes (available in craft shops) you can produce leaves, for example, very quickly and effortlessly for decoration purposes. To obtain a leaf imprint, roll out the clay thinly, cut out the leaves on the work surface to the required size and press briefly with the metal plate. Remove the plate and dust the leaves generously with bronze powder.   This brings out the grain very nicely. Decorating these shapes with appropriately sized diamanté stones gives your brooch a particularly high-quality look. (A pair of tweezers will make this operation a lot easier.)

   Whenever you use modelling clay to mould leaves, strips, or flowers which are to be incorporated into the piece of jewellery, the front needs to be bronzed separately on the work surface; dust generously with the required shade of bronze powder before sticking in position. This makes varnishing easier after hardening. Your piece is now ready for the oven.

Order of working

The following order of working is suggested as a basic guideline for constructing all the pieces of jewellery in this section.

   First of all, assemble all the materials you need for your piece of jewellery.   Then mix only a small quantity of the epoxy adhesive – i.e. binder and setting agent – for the following work stages, as it sets very quickly. Using something like a tooth-pick, spread a little glue on the brooch-base and then press the modelling material immediately into place, carefully smoothing it down with a finger. Cut off any protruding clay with a sharp knife. If you want to incorporate any decorative chains, do that next. Press the decorative chains into the bottom edge of the brooch-base.   In the case of a belt fastener or something similar, press it into the clay and then apply some more clay over it to make sure that it stays in place.   You can create an effective background by taking, for example, a toothbrush or a tea-strainer and pressing it into the clay or rubbing it across the surface.   Trim a No. 4 paintbrush to achieve a blunt edge and apply a very thin layer of bronze powder evenly over the textured clay. Lastly, harden and varnish the piece.

Using moulded decorative features.

INDIVIDUAL PIECES

Small treasures

'Small is beautiful' is the motto here. Medium-length and short necklaces are particularly suitable for blouses with a low neckline, or you can use a longer chain for an afternoon or cocktail dress. A compact brooch looks very good on the lapel of a suit or blazer.

Materials Small oval blanks for pendants; oval brooch-blanks; faceted mirror-backed glass stones; a pair of oval blanks for clip-on earrings; various gilt decorative chains and spring catches; small diamanté stones and metal beads; small gold balls.

Method This jewellery is made as described in the general instructions on pages 48–51.

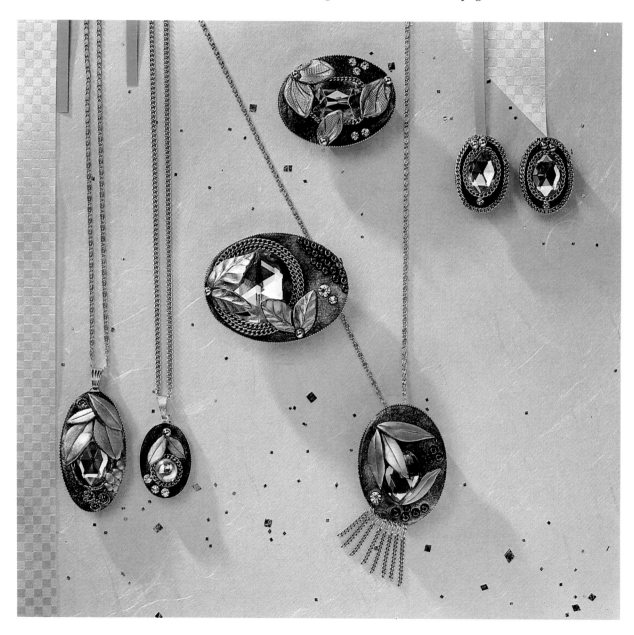

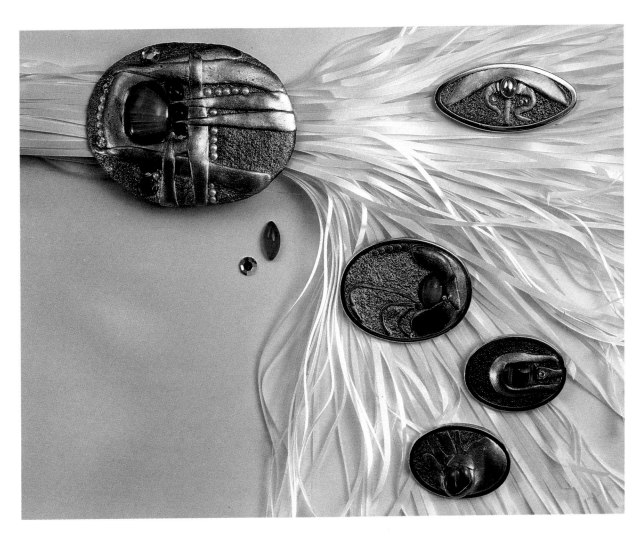

A hint of the exotic

Materials Glass stones; beads; diamanté stones; brooch-blanks; belt fastener; modelling clay; various powders.

Method For the belt fastener, use black modelling clay for the base; use a toothbrush to add texture. Press a glass stone into place. Roll out a lump of clay and place around the stone (see left in picture). Use different-sized pieces of rolled-out modelling clay and press beads, diamanté stones, and glass stones into place; colour with olive-green and gold-bronze powder. Varnish after hardening and stick the fastener on to the back. For the brooches, work black clay into each of the brooch-bases. Use a toothbrush to add texture to the surface of each brooch before positioning stones and decoration. Press the stones into place. Decorate with rolled-out 'sausages' of varying lengths and thicknesses, and colour with grey, navy-blue, gold, purple, olive-green, and gold-bronze powder. Varnish after the hardening process.

Tips It is a good idea to use a porcelain plate as a work-surface. You can then put the finished pieces along with the plate directly into the oven. The pieces with a metal base should also be carefully secured with an all-purpose glue after the hardening process. Through coming into contact with your skin the bronze powder or the eye-shadow could discolour, so to avoid this, apply several coats of the special clear varnish. Not all stones, glass stones, beads, or synthetic products can withstand heat. Their appearance could alter; they could even melt. So watch the temperature – put the oven on a lower setting rather than one that is too high.

Prestige pieces

Others will almost certainly be envious of these belts, which are works of art. Making them, however, does demand quite a lot of time and effort.

Materials A plain leather belt approx 3cm (1¼in) wide (e.g. a man's belt); a large flat disc of mother-of-pearl; white and bright-yellow glass stones; a shaped belt made from imitation lizard skin; a large faceted and mirror-backed glass stone (white); two smaller smooth glass stones (white); five small diamanté stones; metal beads and gold-coloured trace chains; for the necklace, a small black kid-leather thong with small adjustable chains; one medium-sized and two small mirror-backed glass stones.

Method For the belt at the top of the picture, roll out a piece of modelling clay to a thickness of about 0.5cm (¼in). Lay a piece of tinfoil, already cut to size (see techniques on page 48), over it and cut out the shape using a sharp kitchen knife. When you remove the tinfoil, add texture to the basic form using a tea-strainer and then attach the chains and the disc of mother-of-pearl. Make the leaves, again using a pattern, colour them in three shades of bronze, and stick them in position, then attach some little clay

snakes to add texture. Finish off with small glass stones arranged to suit your taste. For the hardening process, lay the complete belt plaque on an old casserole dish so that it will have the proper curve to fit the body. After hardening and sufficient cooling, varnish it twice whilst it is still on the casserole dish. Before sticking it on to the leather belt (use special leather glue), roughen the back of the belt plaque and the corresponding part of the belt with sandpaper. Leave to dry for as long as possible (overnight). The belt in the bottom half of the picture is made in the same way. If the leather belt and the artificial leather belt are already the right shape they do not need to be cut. Stick the plaque made from clay in position before decorating it and place the whole belt on the casserole dish in the oven to harden at 90°C (190°F) for about thirty minutes. For the necklace, roll out a piece of clay to about 1cm (½in) thick and cut out a banana shape. Press the leather thong into the back of the necklace plaque and glue it securely. Texturize the front, using the tea-strainer again, and complete the piece with leaves, stones, bronze powder, and varnish.

The unusual and the extravagant

Materials An oval combined chain and brooch-base; gold-coloured double layer of black kid-leather thongs; a large oval brooch-base with decorative edge, gold-coloured; a silver-coloured belt fastener with 4cm-wide (1½in) carriers; navy-blue elasticated belt, 4cm (1½in) wide; two thin fluted gold-coloured fashion-jewellery bangles; flat silver-coloured trace chains (sold by the metre/yard); small diamanté stones; various shades of eye-shadow; a brandy glass and a cocktail glass.

Method For these pieces of jewellery, apply glue to the bases and put in more clay than usual to produce a slightly raised appearance. After smoothing this over with a finger, use a brandy glass to make even curved indentations in the brooches and a larger glass (the cocktail glass) for the belt fastener. Divide the bangle into different-sized pieces with pliers and

stick them on to the brooches. For the belt fastener, use pieces of silver-coloured trace chain too. With the toothbrush, roughen all the centre sections of the pieces of jewellery and finally stick the diamanté stones into position. Finish the pieces off using eye-shadow and various bronze powders, then harden and varnish them.

Imaginative belts

Materials Gold-coloured belt-bases with 4cm-wide (1½in) carriers; elasticated belt, 4cm (1½in) wide; a combined, gold-coloured brooch with chains; gold-coloured decorative chains; small diamanté stones and gold beads; a pink faceted and mirror-backed glass stone; two small glass stones; one large and one small oval synthetic stone (imitation onyx); a piece of mother-of-pearl.

Method Both of these belts are made using the tricolour technique (see page 51). To get the netting effect on the black belt, use a tea-strainer. To provide additional support and decoration for the small chains, press small balls of clay into position and dust them with gold powder. The necklace shown in the picture would complement the black belt and is made in a similar way.

This jewellery set is just as beautiful worked in silver and using black stones.

Distinguished and discreet

Whether toning with the colour of clothing or acting as a contrast to black, the delicate shades of lilac add a discreet note to casual or elegant fashions.

Materials A bangle; an oval brooch; an oval bracelet with border; a pendant for a chain; a spring bail; decorative trace chain; anchor chain; modelling clay in black, purple, and lilac; gold powder; matt varnish.

Method For the bangle, knead together all three colours of clay. Roll into a long thin sausage shape, about 20cm (8in) in length. Press this evenly into the bangle and join the ends together so that the join does not show. Cut away any excess clay using the knife.

Smooth over the remaining layer several times with thumb and forefinger alternately. The trace chain pressed into either side gives the bangle a discreet touch. Lightly applied gold powder neutralizes the mixed colours. Use the same colours of clay to make the bracelet, oval pendant, and brooch. Use decorative trace chains to mark dividing lines between the colours and apply gold powder sparingly to give all the pieces a silky shimmer.

Use matt varnish after the hardening process, but do not varnish the outer rims of the fittings.

Sunrays

The simple contrast offered by olive-green and white makes a lovely change from coloured designs. Chains set in a pattern of sun-like rays, combined with the softening effect of gold powder, produce interesting and eye-catching pieces.

Materials A decorative pendant; a spring bail; a belt fastener; a brooch with decorative edging; a teardrop-shaped pendant; an ear-wire; an oval spacer ring; a trace chain; two different-sized decorative trace chains; modelling clay in olive-green and white; gold powder; matt varnish.

Method Press olive-green modelling clay into place. Using a knife, cut out a semicircle. Press the white modelling clay into this space. Remove any excess clay with a knife and smooth over the surface with your finger. First of all, cover up the joins between the olive-green and the white clay using small chains. Then press decorative trace chains into the clay in a sunray pattern. Take care to start off each time with a complete chain link. A thin skewer or toothpick will help you to inlay the chains. Apply gold powder to the white clay, smoothing it over with your index finger to get a marbled effect. After hardening the pieces, apply matt varnish (remember not to varnish the metal findings).

Modelled and decorated

Here is another set which has been created using delicate diamanté stones. Unusual in design and accentuated by a fine gold shimmer, these pieces make very special accessories for elegant evening wear.

Materials A brooch-base with decorative edging; a teardrop-shaped pendant blank; two teardrop-shaped earring blanks; two ear-wires; a spring bail; two oval rings; five drop-shaped settings for diamanté; diamanté in three different sizes; trace chains; decorative trace chains; white modelling clay; gold powder; matt varnish; crystal glue.

Method Decorate the teardrop-shaped decorative findings with the corresponding diamanté stones, using only crystal glue. To make the brooch, knead the modelling clay thoroughly. Press into place and remove the upper layer with a knife. Now press the decorative parts you have already prepared into place in a symmetrical fashion. Between both of these elements press alternately trace chains and decorative trace chains in an S-shape. Apply a little gold powder and create an indentation inside the drop-shaped form by pressing your fingertip down in a circular motion. This also creates the marbled effect. (Use too little rather than too much gold powder).

Make the pendant and the earrings in the same way.

After the hardening process, apply matt varnish with a small brush, avoiding the diamanté.

Masks – always in fashion

Metal masks from craft shops lend a very special air to your jewellery. According to the size and shape of your piece of jewellery you can incorporate one or two masks.

Materials Earring blanks with shepherd's-crook ear-wires; various brooch-blanks; a choker with a V-shaped front; large and small metal masks; a metal hand; large and small diamanté stones; beads; trace chain for necklace.

Method Stick the metal masks and hands on to the modelling clay.

With the earrings, the special touch is the tricolour effect of the background (see tricolour technique on page 51). The top section is coloured with antique gold, the middle section with pewter, and the bottom section with copper powder. You can put these together to make a complete set.

60

Painted glass jewellery

Everyone is instantly captivated by the brilliance of glass jewellery. This section deals with the long-established technique of painting on the back of glass. It is now possible to buy special paints and frames with glass inserts cut exactly to size for brooches, earrings, and other pieces of jewellery. Only by experimenting over a period of time will you discover the full range of possibilities for these new paints and the wide range of creations they can give rise to. Fantastic forms are often discovered accidentally, but you can also set out with a particular creative idea in mind. The examples and tips in this section are intended to make it easier for you to start working with this fascinating technique.

The great advantage of this technique is that you can experiment at your leisure; if a creation works you can frame it; if it does not, you can simply wash it off with water and start again. Have fun experimenting with the different paints and working on your creations.

BASIC MATERIALS AND TECHNIQUES

Materials

Frames for jewellery with glass inserts; texturizing paste; pearly lustre; foundation; glitter paints; gutta; various special-effect papers; modelling clay.

Equipment

Transparent plastic film; plastic bottle with fine nozzle; darning needle or large ordinary needle; sheet of glass to use as work surface; black paper or card; hair dryer; tumbler of water; domestic oven; possibly a palette.

Techniques

Applying texturizing paste The glass slide for the brooch must be clean and thoroughly dry before you apply any texturizing paste from the tube. Lay a piece of plastic film over it and smooth down the paste with your finger. If you press your finger down harder, you can clear the paste from certain spots and thereby create shapes (such as circles or leaves). Finally, lift off the plastic film and leave the structures to dry on the slide.

Peeling back the plastic film from the texturizing paste.

Working with glitter paint For the next step you can use glitter paint if you like. You can apply the paint straight from the tube or with a paintbrush. To draw thinner lines, use a plastic bottle with a fine nozzle. Using a brush dipped in water, you can move the glitter particles into the required position. When the whitish-coloured paste has gone transparent the glitter paint is dry.

Applying glitter paints with a fine nozzle.

Pearly lustre Pearly lustre needs to be shaken or stirred well before using. Then wait until any bubbles arising during shaking have disappeared. Now you can apply the pearly lustre with the brush, applying different colours next to one another or dropping them one colour inside another. If you want the effect of colours running into one another, you need to apply the colours quickly or drying edges may prevent the colours from running. You can only control the application and running of pearly lustre on a black background. The pearly lustre needs to be completely dry before you continue.

Applying pearly lustre.

as evenly as possible. Dry the first coat with a hair dryer and repeat this procedure twice more until the paint completely covers the glass. Black foundation can be used for decorative purposes as well as merely for coating the glass.

Assembly When the colours are completely dry, lay the glass slide, unpainted side down, in the frame. Attach the brooch-back and bend over the claws to secure everything in the frame.

Rejects If you are not completely happy with a piece of jewellery, do not wash the painting off straight away: try leaving it in water for a quarter of an hour. The paints will lift off the glass slide like a skin and can be pushed around and pushed together to form shapes on the slide which can sometimes be very effective. When dry, the paints will stick fast to the glass slide again.

Foundation You can only see the true brilliance of the pearly lustre after you have coated it with black foundation. To prevent mishaps when applying the foundation, do not apply the coats too thickly or you will get cracks and irregularities forming. The following method is very reliable: first of all, water down the foundation a little. Then apply the foundation, each stroke lying side by side with the next, making sure that the foundation layer is applied

Rejects.

Above, you can see two of these rejects. Using pearly lustre, small trees have been painted on the larger, square brooch. For the rectangular brooch, after carrying out the above procedure, some silver glitter particles (bottom left) and the rounded pearly-lustre shape (bottom right) were added. Finally, the brooches were coated with black foundation.

Applying foundation.

63

INDIVIDUAL PIECES

Glittering pieces of jewellery

Materials See the general list on page 62.

Method For the large square brooch (top), first of all draw the tree and its roots using gold glitter paint and leave to dry. Then coat the upper half and the delicate golden roots with black foundation. Now apply a little blue glitter paint to the bottom half and arrange the individual glitter particles using a brush dipped in water. Finally, coat all the roots in white foundation. As a variation, you could push the glitter particles around with the brush so that some of the particles are isolated and others grouped together. For the oval brooch (bottom left), black foundation was used as well as white.

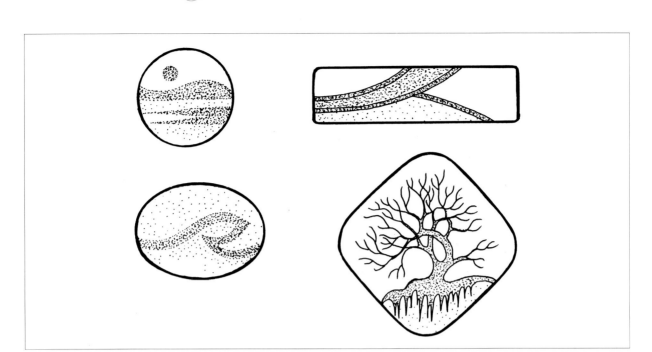

Outline diagrams for the jewellery designs in the picture on page 64. The diagrams are shown in reverse to aid tracing off.

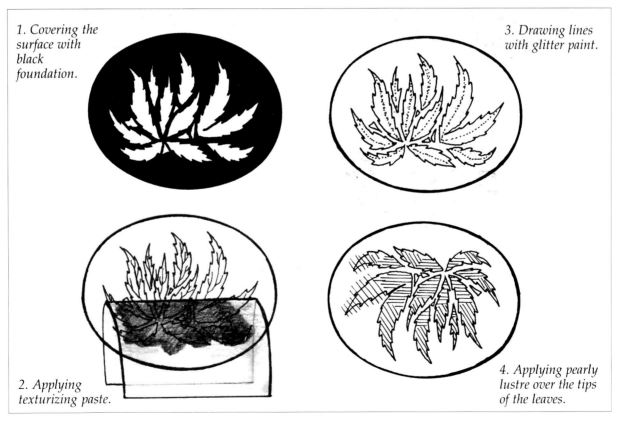

1. Covering the surface with black foundation.

3. Drawing lines with glitter paint.

2. Applying texturizing paste.

4. Applying pearly lustre over the tips of the leaves.

Outline diagrams for the leaf brooch pictured on page 66, showing the stages of construction.

Keeping black until last

Materials See the general list on page 62.

Method With the two brooches shown close together on the left, it is hard to tell at first glance that black foundation was applied first. (You could get the same effect, though, if you applied the black foundation as the final stage.) The large round brooch, however, shows that the technique of keeping the black until the final stage makes it easier to work with the glass. Use a razor blade on the black foundation to achieve the desired effect, and scratch out the shapes of the jagged and pointed leaves using a darning needle. All the other materials are applied in the order already described on pages 62–3.

The fascinating world of flowers

Materials See the general list on page 62.

Method Flower motifs are produced by scratching shapes out of the black background and backing them with special-effect papers. You can get a particularly impressive effect by using pearly lustre on certain sections of the picture. When the pearly lustre has dried, paint over any details you have used it on with black foundation, as precisely and uniformly as possible. Use purple, blue, and copper pearly lustre to paint the pansies on the oval brooch. The leaves on the different brooches appear golden or green in colour according to the type of backing

paper used: for the marguerites, for example, use a small piece of shiny green ribbon to give colour to the engraved leaves. Paint the petals of the marguerites with white foundation, and their centres with yellow poster paint.

Back the stamens and leaves of the columbine (see above – top left) with rainbow-effect paper, and use silver and purple for the petals. The dandelion clocks (see above – top) are particularly attractive if the downy heads are finely and delicately engraved. (Use an ordinary needle – the darning needle is too blunt). The silvery effect on the seed heads comes from a small piece of silver crêpe. Paint the leaves with blue pearly lustre in places. The golden sun is echoed by the gilt brooch-frame.

The effect of the purple imaginary flowers (painted with pearly lustre) in the large round brooch (far left in the picture on page 67) is enhanced by a small piece of gold crêpe behind.

Outline diagrams for the jewellery designs shown on page 67.

Outline diagrams for the jewellery designs shown on page 69. Scratch out the areas shaded black.

Jewellery ideas with a personal touch

If you like precise work and have a steady hand, these designs are certainly worth trying.

Materials See the general list on page 62.

Method Scratch out the designs in the brooches in the right-hand half of the picture and back them with pieces of different gold-coloured, shiny wrapping paper or gift ribbon. Only the windows and doors of the oriental city should be painted with blue pearly lustre. For the leaves on the rectangular brooch, apply blue and purple in quick succession, and paint the raindrops in the choker pendant in blue and gold shades, accentuating their fine nuances by applying different amounts of each colour and mixing the colours together. So that the colours on the drops do not run uncontrollably into one another, leave hairline foundation lines as outlines. For the other two pieces of jewellery, use brightly coloured rainbow paper as a background. This gives you the fine nuances of colour on the round cupolas on the mosque, the decorative lines that run beneath it, and the narrow leaves of the allium. Scratch out the flower-heads of the allium and fill them in with blue and purple pearly lustre and a mixture of these two colours.

Star signs

Star signs are always popular as motifs for items of jewellery. These examples are distinctly elegant and delicate as a result of the fine ornamental work and the glowing colour of the liquid bronze.

Materials Brooch-frames with glass inserts and metal bases; black foundation; 'fine-gold' liquid bronze; paintbrush; darning needle or ordinary needle; cotton-wool buds.

Method First of all, coat the glass with black foundation. Then, using a darning needle or a large ordinary needle, scratch out the outlines of the star signs. You can mark these out first in pencil on the black foundation or trace them on using carbon paper. (See opposite for outline diagrams of all twelve star signs). When you have the outlines in place, start by decorating the inner areas with little patterns: teardrops, zigzags, circles – you can incorporate any design feature you like. For such fine work the darning needle is too thick, so use an ordinary needle. After engraving the picture, dab on the liquid bronze using a cotton-wool bud. When it is dry, hold it up to the light to see if the bronze looks thin at any point, so that you can touch it up.

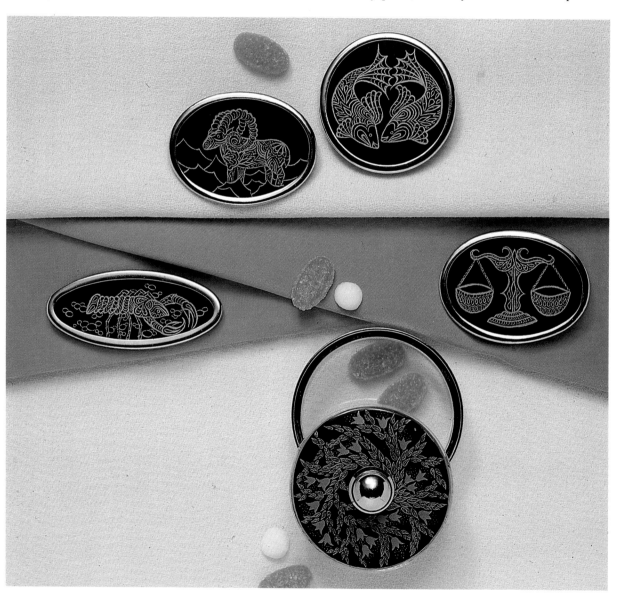

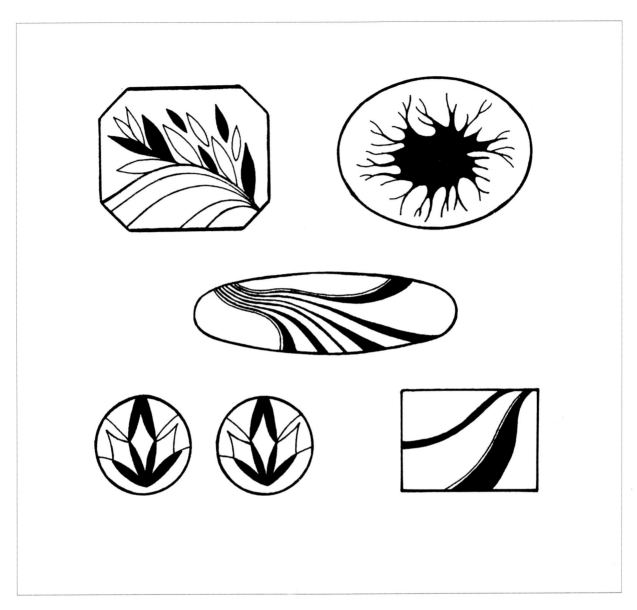

Outline diagrams for all the pieces of jewellery on page 74 – actual size.

Method First of all, dip the toothbrush in the paint and run it across the sieve, spraying the paint through the sieve and on to the glass slide beneath. Spray the shades of colour one after another on to the glass slide until the whole surface area is covered. Make sure that there is not too much paint on the toothbrush (otherwise the droplets will be too big) and also that there are gaps between the individual speckles of paint. After it has dried, make lines and areas in the spattered finish using an engraving pen, then paint behind the sprayed sections using gold pearly lustre (or silver for the octagonal brooch) and paint thin gold lines in pearly lustre on some of the edges. For the large oval brooch, paint the small leaves in greenish-blue pearly lustre, using a fine brush, and link the leaves up with golden branches.

In all cases the final stage is to coat them with black foundation. Then embed the glass slide (as described on page 73) in the modelling clay to make a frame. After the hardening process, apply a little onyx-glitter to the frames, and, finally, clear matt varnish for protection.

Brooches with watch parts

You can always find things which are attractive enough in shape or colour to be integrated into a brooch.

Small, flat watch parts like the ones you can buy in craft shops are particularly fascinating. The method is simple and the result captivating, particularly the effective contrast between the rigid geometric forms of the watch parts and the free, flowing forms of the painting. A further variation is possible by sticking larger watch parts to the brooch-frame using epoxy adhesive.

Materials Brooch-frames with glass inserts and metal bases; various watch parts; glass stones; texturizing paste; glitter paints in silver and blue; pearly lustre in blue, green, purple, copper, and silver; black foundation; plastic film; paintbrush; epoxy adhesive.

Method For the oval brooches, apply the texturizing paste more thickly than usual and distribute it with the help of the plastic film in a horizontal direction by pressing lightly with your fingers. Peel off the film towards the right. Then lay the watch parts on the damp paste and press them gently into place. Proceed carefully at this point to retain the finely branched effect. The parts must not be positioned too loosely or later on any paint applied will run between the paste and the watch parts. (Of course, you can use this as a creative technique, for often the unintentional and random aspect of the work process produces the most charming results.) When the texturizing paste has dried, carry on working as usual with glitter paints and pearly lustre.

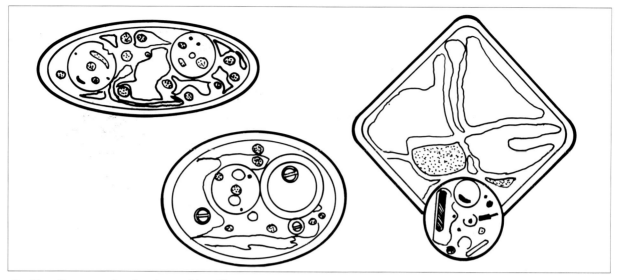

Outline diagrams for the pieces of jewellery on page 76: actual size.

For the square brooch (left in the picture on page 76), do not inset any watch parts into it; instead, stick a somewhat larger part on to the frame plus two glass stones, using a rapid-action epoxy adhesive. (Please follow the manufacturers' instructions.)

To make the picture on the square brooch, apply texturizing paste generously and stroke it from top to bottom using a plastic film. Finally, peel off the film from two corners simultaneously towards the centre to get the ridge on the central axis. Continue with the usual procedure.

More watch-part brooches

Watch parts are inset in these three brooches (see picture on page 78) as well as being stuck on the frame. A new material is used for the square brooch: gold leaf.

Materials Brooch-frames with glass inserts and metal bases; watch parts; glass stones; gold leaf in sheet form; texturizing paste; glitter paints in silver and iris; pearly lustre in gold, green, purple, blue, and

Outline diagrams for the pieces of jewellery on page 78: actual size.

77

copper; black foundation; plastic film; paintbrush; cotton-wool buds; epoxy adhesive.

Method The oval and semicircular brooches are produced using the same technique as for the previous examples. The square brooch also has small pieces of gold leaf. First of all, create texture using paste and inset the watch parts into the still-damp clay. After drying, apply the pearly-lustre colour of your choice as a bonding agent, lay the sheet of gold leaf with the backing paper (gold side down) over it, and press gently with the cotton-wool buds in different places on the backing paper. In these places the gold leaf will remain stuck to the liquid pearly lustre when you peel off the backing paper. Allow to dry and carry on in the usual fashion: bring out the main features with glitter paint and paint the texturized parts with pearly lustre. Finally, coat everything with black foundation.

Playing with colours

These five brooches show how harmoniously the motifs, colours, and shapes of jewellery can complement one another.

Materials Brooch-frames with glass inserts and metal bases; texturizing paste; glitter paints in gold, silver, and iris; pearly lustre in green, red, copper, and blue; black foundation; plastic film; paintbrush.

Method For all five brooches, first of all apply texturizing paste; then lay plastic film over it and stroke the paste in different directions, applying varying degrees of pressure with your fingers. Be sure not to cover the whole surface of the glass with paste – leave room for a background. Against a black background the coloured shapes appear more three-dimensional and the colours more vibrant. After drying, apply glitter paints to the places on the texturizing paste which looked very thin when you removed the film. For the triangular brooch in the centre, use iris and silver glitter paints, and for the others, gold or silver, according to the frame. Then paint the rest of the paste formations using pearly lustre, and, finally, apply a coat of black foundation.

Index